Time to Eat

by Barbara L. Luciano
illustrated by Ginna Magee

PEARSON

Scott
Foresman

Editorial Offices: Glenview, Illinois • Parsippany, New Jersey • New York, New York
Sales Offices: Needham, Massachusetts • Duluth, Georgia • Glenview, Illinois
Coppell, Texas • Sacramento, California • Mesa, Arizona

Every effort has been made to secure permission and provide appropriate credit for photographic material. The publisher deeply regrets any omission and pledges to correct errors called to its attention in subsequent editions.

Unless otherwise acknowledged, all photographs are the property of Scott Foresman, a division of Pearson Education.

Photo locators denoted as follows: Top (T), Center (C), Bottom (B), Left (L), Right (R), Background (Bkgd)

Illustrations by Ginna Magee

Photograph 8 Corbis

ISBN: 0-328-13151-2

6 7 8 9 10 V010 14 13 12 11 10 09 08 07

The horses eat this dinner.

The chicks eat this dinner.

The pig eats this dinner.

Mom is looking at her watch.

Mom and I eat dinner too.

Animals on the Move

All the animals in this book eat. All the animals can move too. Animals have different ways to move. Some animals walk on feet. Some animals use fins to swim. Some animals even hop! What other ways can animals move?